Cover illustration: USS *Lunga Point* (CVE-94) was one of dozens of US-built escort carriers that saw service in the Second World War. Known also as 'jeep carriers' or 'Woolworth's carriers', these ships were turned out at a frantic pace and served in a wide variety of roles and theatres. A TBM Avenger wheels away after a low pass over the flight deck.

1. Converted from battlecruiser hulls, the two aircraft carriers of the *Lexington* class provided the US Navy with the opportunity to explore the operating procedures that would be put to devastating use during the Second World War. This is a prewar view of *Lexington* (CV-2); her sister-ship *Saratoga* (CV-3), lies at the adjacent berth (left of photo).

Warships Illustrated No 8

The World's Aircraft Carriers 1914-1945

ROGER CHESNEAU

ARMS AND ARMOUR PRESS

Introduction

Published in 1986 by Arms & Armour Press Ltd.,
2–6 Hampstead High Street, London NW3 1QQ.

Distributed in the United States by Sterling
Publishing Co. Inc., 2 Park Avenue, New York,
N.Y. 10016.

British Library Cataloguing in Publication Data:
Chesneau, Roger
The world's aircraft carriers, 1914–1945.
– (Warships illustrated; 8)
1. Aircraft carriers – History
I. Title
623.8′225′0904   V874

ISBN 0-85368-768-4

Editing, design and artwork by Roger Chesneau.
Typesetting by Typesetters (Birmingham) Ltd.
Printed and bound in Italy by GEA/GEP in
association with Keats European Ltd., London.

Aircraft first went to sea in 1913, a mere ten years after sustained, manned flight had first been successfully demonstrated by the Wright Brothers. True, the carrier concerned was an old cruiser and in reality acted as little more than a means of transport for its frail cargo, but its concept laid the foundations for what was literally a new dimension in maritime power. The First World War witnessed astonishing strides in naval aviation, so much so that by its close the layout of the aircraft carrier as it exists today had already been established and the roles for its aircraft had already been clearly defined: the evolution of the ship type over the last seventy years or so has been mainly concerned with changes of emphasis, technological improvement and, of course, a tremendous growth in both ship size and capabilities.

This volume takes a brief look at the development of the aircraft carrier from its formative years through to the close of the Second World War, by which time it had proved beyond all doubt its position as the most powerful and versatile asset a navy could possess. The year 1945 marked a watershed in the history of naval aviation in another sense, for towards the close of that year the first landing aboard ship by a jet-powered aircraft took place, an event wich would have far-reaching implications for carrier design. The illustrations reflect the expedient nature of the earliest ships, the use put in the 1920s to surplus capital ships hulls and the gradual crystallization of operating experience in the purpose-built carriers of the 1930s and 1940s.

The photographs in this book come from the US Navy, the US Naval Historical Center, the US National Archives, the Ministry of Defence (Navy), the Fleet Air Arm Museum, Toshio Imachi, Boeing, Shell Tankers (UK) Ltd, Bernard Millot and the author's collection. For a more detailed discussion of the subject of aircraft carriers the reader is referred to the author's *Aircraft Carriers of the World, 1914 to the Present: An Illustrated Encyclopedia.*

Roger Chesneau

◀2
2. With the outbreak of the Second World War, the desperate clamour for extra aircraft carriers led to the commissioning of huge numbers of ships whose hulls were originally designed for totally different roles. A batch of vessels first laid down as *Cleveland* class cruisers emerged in 1943 as *Independence* class light carriers; one such, *San Jacinto* (CVL-30), is shown.

▲3

3. The first aircraft carrier specifically employed as such was the British converted ex-cruiser *Hermes*, which, equipped with a flying-off platform, protective canvas shelters and handling derricks, took two or three aircraft to sea during the July 1913 Naval Manoeuvres. The object was to provide spotting and reconnaissance facilities, but bad weather prevented the aircraft from being flown. Shortly after the outbreak of the First World War the ship was torpedoed and sunk by a German submarine; the photo shows her foundering.

4. Aircraft carriers went to war as early as December 1914, when seven seaplanes operating from three carriers attacked Cuxhaven on Christmas Day. One of the ships taking part was *Engadine*, a converted cross-channel packet. The canvas shelters on the forecastle and shelter deck and the heightened bridge structure represent the sum total of the modifications made at this stage.

▼4

5. Laid down as a collier/grain carrier, *Ark Royal*, commissioned in December 1914, is regarded by many as the first true aircraft carrier: certainly she was equipped with comprehensive maintenance facilities for her complement of seven seaplanes. Her long flying-off deck forward permitted her to operate landplanes as well, and in later years, renamed *Pegasus*, she saw service as a catapult trials ship. She was still in use as a depot ship in 1945.

6. *Ben-My-Chree*, commissioned in early 1915, was another steam packet requisitioned by the Admiralty. Modifications were more extensive than those initially applied to her predecessors, and included a rigid seaplane hangar (note the Short 184s within), topped by 3pdr anti-aircraft guns, and a pair of 12pdrs on the stern.

▲7

7. *Vindex*, again an ex-packet, had split foremasts to enable the length of her bow launching ramp to be maximized. The ramp, a feature of several other early carriers, was fitted to enable wheeled aircraft to take off from the ship, but in practice sea conditions frequently rendered it unusable.

8. Japan quickly appreciated the potential of air-capable ships, and her first carrier, *Wakamiya*, was commissioned in the summer of 1914. A former cargo vessel, she could carry four seaplanes beneath canvas hangars fitted on her well decks. Her capabilities were demonstrated a few months after she entered service, when her aircraft bombed and sank a German minelayer at Tsingtao.

9. 'Quick-fix' conversions of merchant ships to enable them to operate aircraft were undertaken by other navies during the early months of the First World War. The French *Campinas* could carry up to eight seaplanes, hoisted out from their hangars by means of derricks.

10. The bow launching ramp of *Campania*, a large ex-Cunard liner modified as an aircraft carrier in 1914–15. Crewmen are positioning a Fairey Campania patrol seaplane – named specifically after the ship for which it was designed – prior to take off, which will be made using wheeled dollies beneath the floats. *Campania* was selected for conversion since she was large enough and fast enough to operate in concert with the battle fleet. Note the split forefunnels and extemporary bridge structure.

▼8

9 ▲   10 ▼

9

▲11　▼12

11. One of the most ambitious aircraft carrier conversions of the
First World War involved the large light battlecruiser *Furious*. Her
forward 18in gun mounting was removed, permitting a capacious
hangar topped by a 228ft flight deck to be installed – a very
considerable improvement over the facilities on existing Royal Navy
carriers. Sqn Cdr Dunning successfully landed a Sopwith Pup on
this deck in mid-1917, although during a later attempt he lost his
life. Before the end of the First World War *Furious* would receive a
second hangar and landing-on deck aft, in which configuration she
carried out the epic raid on the Zeppelin sheds at Tondern.
12. An aerial view of *Pegasus*, last of the Royal Navy's early-
generation seaplane carriers, in a striking 'dazzle' camouflage
scheme. The main features of the layout are clearly seen: inclined
flying-off deck forward; hangar and cranes aft. A Fairey Campania
sits on the quarterdeck.

13. The problem facing aviators trying to land on board ship was a
basic one: how to avoid the vessel's superstructure. *Argus*, originally
designed as an Italian liner, tackled the issue in a fundamental way.
Her uptakes were led aft to discharge at the stern and navigation
was facilitated by means of conning positions port and starboard
(below the level of the fully flush flight deck) and a retractable
charthouse forward. Accepted by the Royal Navy in 1918, the ship
went on to serve with distinction during the Second World War.
14. *Vindictive*, commissioned at about the same time as *Argus*, was
a converted cruiser intended, like *Furious*, to operate with the
battle fleet's scouting screen, providing aerial reconnaissance. This
early photograph shows the 215ft after flight deck above the main
hangar, with crash barrier rigged abaft the second funnel. The
carrier retained four of her original seven 7.5in low-angle guns.

▲15

16▲

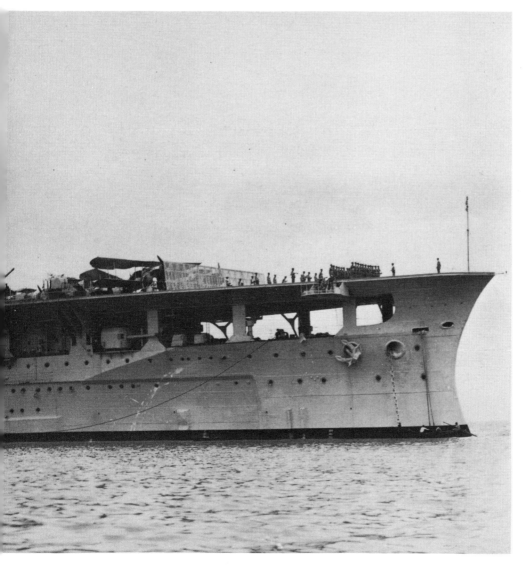

◀17

15. *Hermes*, launched in 1919, was the Royal Navy's first carrier designed from the outset as such. She was innovative in several respects, not least in her 'island' superstructure which, offset to starboard, has become a standard carrier design feature. For most of her service life she was stationed in the Far East, and she was sunk by Japanese aircraft in April 1942.

16. Somewhat larger than *Hermes*, *Eagle* utilized the hull and machinery of a Chilean dreadnought battleship requisitioned by the Admiralty. She entered service in early 1924, having previously been involved in extensive flying trials. This photograph was taken shortly afterwards.

17. *Eagle* in 1938–39, with Swordfish torpedo-spotter-reconnaissance biplanes on deck. The carrier's low-angle, anti-ship 6in guns were complemented by 4in AA weapons and, prior to the outbreak of war, by 2pdr 'pompoms'. *Eagle* was sunk by torpedoes in the Mediterranean in 1942.

▲18 ▼19

18. Japan's first true aircraft carrier, *Hosho*, was commissioned in late 1922 and was one of the very few Japanese warships to survive the Second World War intact. With a standard displacement of around 7,500 tons, she was a small vessel by carrier standards, and was employed mainly in training duties. This view shows her forecastle, above which rise deck-edge stanchions supporting the flight deck, and is dated October 1945.

19. The Japanese carrier *Notoro* operated during the 1920s and 1930s with a complement of seaplanes (visible here on the covered well decks) but retained her primary capabilities as an oiler. She saw combat during the Sino-Japanese War of 1937.

20. A Douglas DT torpedo-bomber departs from the US Navy's first aircraft carrier (CV-1), the ship's name boldly proclaimed on the biplane's fuselage. *Langley* was another converted merchantman, in this instance a collier, and was flush-decked, her boilers discharging via hinged funnels at the deck edge. Cargo vessels such as these were particularly suited for modification to carriers since their capacious holds could be adapted to function as hangars.

21. The Washington Treaty of 1922 resulted in the cancellation of a large number of US, British and Japanese 'super-dreadnoughts'; some of these had already been laid down, and their hulls conveniently formed the basis for programmes of carrier construction. In the United States, two such ships, *Lexington* and *Saratoga*, emerged in 1927: at 38,500 tons (standard) displacement, and with an overall length of nearly 900ft, they were the largest carriers in the world until the end of the Second World War. This is *Saratoga* (CV-3), May 1929, with a pair of O2U observation aircraft flying over.

20 ▲   21 ▼

▲ 22 ▼ 23

22. A close view of *Saratoga*'s bows. The hull plating was carried right up to the flight deck – a design feature that would disappear from US carriers until the post-Second World War reconstruction programmes.

23. F4B-4 fighters ranged on board *Saratoga* in the early 1930s. Visible in front of the island is one of the ship's four twin 8in gun mountings; anti-surface weapons such as these were fitted to many early fleet aircraft carriers, the main intention being to combat enemy cruisers.

24. The first large Japanese aircraft carrier was *Akagi*, shown here in about 1930. The small island visible on the starboard edge of the flight deck was a temporary affair, a permanent structure not being fitted until the ship was fully reconstructed in the mid-1930s. This carrier would lead the Pearl Harbor strike force in December 1941.

25. *Kaga* was somewhat smaller than *Akagi* but, like her, was converted from a capital ship hull. She was one of several carriers to be fitted with 'stepped' flight decks forward, to enable extra aircraft to be flown off (or some aircraft to be flown off while others were returning).

24 ▲   25 ▼

▲ 26

26. Ex-battlecruiser hulls provided for large aircraft capacity and high speed; battleship hulls, generally designed for battle-fleet speeds of around 23kts and much more strongly constructed, were less than ideal although still attractive. Like the Royal Navy's *Eagle*, the French *Béarn* was built on one of the latter – she was originally laid down as a 25,000-ton, 13.4in-gunned dreadnought.

27. *Béarn* in the mid-1930s. A major problem facing aircraft carrier designers was how to get rid of boiler gases. Some opted for horizontal discharge below flight-deck level, but most (including *Béarn*'s) led the uptakes into a deck-edge funnel, located close to, or even combined with, the island superstructure.

28. Apart from *Furious*, there were two other large light cruisers (often referred to as battlecruisers) on the Royal Navy's inventory, and following the Washington Treaty it was decided to convert them to aircraft carriers. *Courageous* (shown) and *Glorious* proved to be the most successful British carriers of the interwar period; they

were fast (over 30kts) and steady, and could accommodate 48 aircraft.

29. In the 1920s *Furious* was further modified by having her midships superstructure razed and a completely flush flight deck installed. The smoke from the boilers was led aft, discharging at the after edges of the flight deck and from the hull side plating below. The ship is shown here recovering one of her aircraft during late 1920s Fleet manoeuvres.

30. The forward edge of *Furious*' flight deck was aerodynamically contoured, to minimize the creation of swirling air currents that might affect aircraft taking off; atop it was a retractable charthouse. Also visible in this late 1920s photograph are the auxiliary flying-off deck ('slip deck') over the bows, the palisades fitted at the edge of the main flight deck (to prevent aircraft from running off) and one of the carrier's 5.5in low-angle guns.

▼ 27

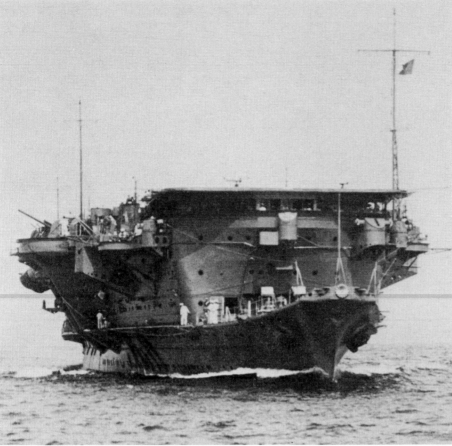

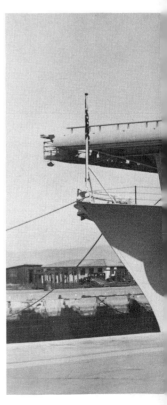

▲31

31. Many carriers featured 'double-deck' hangars in order to get more aircraft aboard, but in the Japanese carrier *Ryujo*, launched in 1931, these caused excessive topweight and stability problems, aggravated by the fact that the ship displaced only 8,000 tons standard. She was built to avoid the constraints of the Washington Treaty, which controlled the building of carriers over 10,000 tons. *Ryujo* had no island, and the bridge was located beneath the forward edge of the flight deck. She was sunk by aircraft from the US carrier *Saratoga* in August 1942.

32. Specialized seaplane carriers continued in service after the First World War, particularly in Japan. *Kamoi*, launched in the early 1920s as an oiler, was converted for the role and entered service in 1933 with the Imperial Japanese Navy, her general arrangement not much different from the earlier *Wakamiya*. This aerial photograph shows her covered well decks and an experimental Hein mat trailed at the stern for recovering her aircraft.

33. The US Navy's first carrier designed from the outset as such was *Ranger* (CV-4), shown here immediately after her launch. She was to have been fitted with a completely flush deck, but a small island superstructure was added before the ship commissioned; her uptakes were, however, led aft to discharge via six hinged funnels. The lifts amidships were offset to starboard to enable aircraft on the flight deck to be moved around them.

34. *Ranger* in March 1937, about three years after her completion. The original scheme to build her as a flush-decked carrier required the bridge to be located beneath the flight deck: it is clearly visible in this photograph.

▼32

▲35 ▼36

37 ▲

35. The culmination of inter-war carrier experience in the Royal Navy was represented by *Ark Royal*, completed in late 1938. Double-storey hangers dictated a high freeboard and enabled sixty aircraft to be accommodated, and anti-aircraft defence, comprising sixteen 4.5in dual-purpose (DP) guns and six 8-barrelled 2pdr 'pompoms', was strong. *Ark Royal* was sunk by a U-boat in November 1941, but not before she had been 'sunk' (according to German propaganda) many times before.

36. On December 1938, amid the usual pomp and ceremony, Germany launched her first aircraft carrier, *Graf Zeppelin*, but as the Second World War unfolded resources were concentrated in other areas and general disenchantment set in, and the ship was never completed. Had she commissioned, she would probably have included navalized Ju 87 ('Stuka') bombers and Messerschmitt Bf 109 fighters in her aircraft complement.

37. The Japanese carriers *Akagi* and *Kaga* were completely reconstructed in the 1930s: the auxiliary flight decks were abandoned, the main flight deck lengthened, the hangars enlarged, the machinery replaced and the armament upgraded. This view of *Kaga* as she appeared in 1936 shows her new lines; particularly evident is her downward-angled funnel amidships.

38. Two powerful Japanese carriers were commissioned in the late 1930s, in breach of Washington regulations. The first of these, *Soryu*, is shown here fitting out, in 1936. Both this vessel and her semi-sister *Hiryu* were fast, well-armed vessels with a good-size aircraft complement, but they were relatively lightly constructed and both would be lost during the Second World War as a result of uncontrollable fires caused by the detonation of three or four bombs.

38 ▼

▲ 39

39. *Hiryu* (shown) and *Soryu* continued the Japanese practice of trunking the uptakes into downward-discharging funnels, so maximizing flight-deck area. Cruiser-like armament was by now abandoned, and the battery of DP and AA guns was located along the edge of the flight deck, below deck level, where the weapons could command good sky arcs.

40. In *Hiryu* and *Soryu*, command and control of the ships were nevertheless still exercised via island superstructures. In *Hiryu* (and *Akagi*) this was located to port instead of to starboard, apparently to facilitate the simultaneous recovery of aircraft when the ships

were operating in concert with their sisters (which they were designed to do). This is *Hiryu*, summer 1939.

41. During the 1930s Japan instituted a programme of 'shadow' warship construction, producing ships that could readily be converted for more effective roles in the event of hostilities. The two *Chitose* class seaplane carriers, for example, commissioned as such, showing a small bridge superstructure forward and a long upper deck aft relieved by a massive aircraft servicing platform. The hangar below could be (and later was) utilized for handling midget submarines. *Chiyoda* is shown.

▼ 40

▼ 41

42 ▲

42. Between 1942 and 1944 both *Chitose* and *Chiyoda* were completely reconstructed as front-line aircraft carriers by trunking the uptakes to starboard, building a 300ft hangar on top of the upper deck and adding a full-length flight deck on top of that. Almost unrecognizable from their previous configuration, as shown in this photograph of *Chitose*, the two ships would be lost in 1944.

43. *Mizuho* was generally similar to the *Chitose*s but, although she did serve both as a seaplane carrier/tender and as a depot ship for midget submarines, she was never completely rejigged as a flush-decked aircraft carrier. She is shown here off Tsingtao in about 1939.

43 ▼

▲44 ▼45

44. *Glorious*, with attendant destroyer, just prior to the Second World War. The 'slip deck' was by this time disused, and a pair of catapults ('accelerators') had been added to the forward edge of the main flight deck. This view shows the carrier's two cruciform lifts; just discernible is the shallow ramp formed by the flight deck near the forward lift, intended to slow landing aircraft.

45. Within two weeks of the outbreak of war, *Courageous* had been sunk by a U-boat in the South-West Approaches, and this dramatic photograph appeared in the national newspapers soon afterwards. Over 500 officers and men – almost half her crew – perished with her.

46. *Zuiho* (shown) and *Shoho* were laid down as submarine depot ships but eventually emerged as aircraft carriers – further instances of the 'shadow' programmes pursued by Japan. At 14,200 tons deep load displacement, they were not large ships, but their destroyer-type machinery gave them a respectable speed of 28kts and they could handle about thirty aircraft.

47. One of the most famous carriers of all – the wartime *Enterprise* (CV-6). Clearly seen in this May 1942 photograph is the US preference for open-sided hangars which could be closed up if required by means of shutters. Among the advantages of this arrangement was that petrol vapour could be ventilated out: the fact that most Japanese carriers did not have this facility would have disastrous consequences. Despite considerable public protest, *Enterprise* was sold for scrap in the late 1950s.

▲ 48

48. US carriers of the late 1930s and early 1940s had their hangars built up over the hull as a lightweight superstructure, as shown in this view of *Hornet* (one of *Enterprise*'s two sister-ships); in contrast, contemporary British carrier design favoured the use of the flight deck as the main strength deck, with the hangars an integral part of the hull structure.

49. Another view of *Hornet*, dated spring 1942. The ship would be sunk at Santa Cruz six months later, but she will always be associated with the daring 'Doolittle raid' of April 1942, when, flying off B-25 Mitchell medium bombers, she struck at Tokyo in reprisal for the Japanese attack on Pearl Harbor.

50. Limited to a displacement of 15,000 tons by the terms of the 1922 Washington Treaty, *Wasp* (CV-7) was generally regarded as an unsuccessful US carrier: in order to embark as many aircraft as possible her designers were forced to install low-power machinery and skimp her protection, so as to save weight and space. She spent much of her wartime career in the Atlantic but shortly after her transfer to the Pacific in mid-1942 she was torpedoed by a Japanese submarine.

51. With the construction of *Ark Royal* well under way, thoughts turned to the next aircraft carrier programme for the Royal Navy, and the result was the four ships of the *Illustrious* class. The two-storey hangar arrangement was rejected in favour of a single, heavily armoured hangar designed to protect the ship's aircraft in the event of attack. *Victorious*, shown, would be the subject of an extensive reconstruction postwar – the only ship of the class to be so modified.

▼ 49

▲52   ▼53

52. *Illustrious* in May 1944, whilst operating as part of the Eastern Fleet; the carrier in the left background is the USS *Saratoga*, with which the British ship operated for a time.

53. *Indomitable*, though externally similar to her three *Illustrious* class sister-ships, reverted to a two-storey hangar arrangement, an additional half-hangar being accommodated beneath the main unit. The price was a reduction in the thickness of the armoured hangar sides from 4½in to 1½in. The ship is shown here with Hawker Sea Hurricanes on deck; three of the aircraft are parked with their tailwheels positioned on outriggers, to give more flight deck space.

54. *Indomitable* in 1941, her forward twin 4.5in DP guns clearly visible at the deck edge. The strength of the *Illustrious* class ships proved its worth on numerous occasions in the Mediterranean and the Far East when the carriers suffered bomb and kamikaze damage which would have caused less well protected ships to be lost. A *Royal Sovereign* class battleship can be seen in the background.

55. As in the 1914–18 war, the requirements of the Second World War meant that great numbers of ships were pressed into service as emergency aircraft carriers, the vast majority of which were adapted from mercantile hulls and were generally (if not always quite appropriately) known as 'escort carriers'. The first of these to be commissioned into the Royal Navy was *Audacity*, which was converted from a captured German cargo ship. Her career lasted but six months, ending when she was torpedoed and sunk off the Iberian peninsula in December 1941.

▲56
56. A gigantic programme of escort carrier construction was initiated by the United States during the spring of 1941, and many of the vessels were supplied to the Royal Navy under Lend-Lease arrangements. The first of these was *Archer*, shown here in early 1943. Unlike *Audacity*, she had a hangar, the extent of which is indicated by the enclosed area aft.

57. *Dasher* was one of three *Avenger* class escort carriers supplied to the Royal Navy from US yards; all three ships took part in Operation 'Torch', the Allied invasion of North Africa in November 1942. The flight decks were wood-planked, and there was a single lift aft, as shown.

▼57

58. Retained by the US Navy, primarily to train Fleet Air Arm pilots in the use of US equipment, *Charger* (CVE-30) was generally similar to the *Avenger*s. These escort carriers were diesel-powered, the exhaust gases being discharged via deck-edge outlets amidships
59. The next batch of US-built escort carriers was the *Sangamon* class, adapted from T3 tankers and retained for use by the US Navy. This 1945 photograph of *Suwannee* (CVE-27) shows the proliferation of anti-aircraft guns (within the deck-edge 'tubs') that characterized all major warships as the Second World War progressed.

▲60   ▼61

60. *Sangamon* herself (CVE-26) as completed. The class were turbine-powered, but the four funnels disposed in pairs at the deck edge right aft were very unobtrusive. As can be seen, the island was a small affair, built out on a platform off the flight deck proper and supported by struts angled out from the hull.

61. Another *Sangamon* class carrier, this time *Chenango* (CVE-28), her flight deck covered in desert-camouflaged P-40s en route to North Africa for 'Torch'. Escort carriers were frequently employed as aircraft transports, especially in the Pacific theatre during the closing stages of the Second World War.

62. The *Bogue* class escort carriers were generally similar to the earlier C3-type conversions (*Avenger* class, *Charger*) but had bigger hangars, larger flight decks, and turbine machinery. Twenty-eight aircraft could be embarked in the combat role, almost double the number carried by the *Avengers*. The US Navy operated eleven *Bogues*; this is *Prince William* (CVE-31), the last of the batch.

62▼

▲63   ▼64

65▲

66▲

63. The *Bogue* class carrier *Barnes* (CVE-20), with a deck-load of P-38 and P-47 aircraft en route to a US Army Air Forces base in the Pacific, June 1943.

64. *Breton* (CVE-23), another *Bogue* class escort carrier, showing her planked flight deck, two lifts and single catapult. The two sponsons at the stern mounted single 5in/38 guns.

65. Japanese carrier construction gathered momentum during the late 1930s, and as war loomed in Europe a pair of large and very fast ships went down the ways. *Shokaku* and *Zuikaku* were both completed in time for the attack on Pearl Harbor, and in the subsequent Pacific campaign the two ships proved more durable than earlier designs. This is *Zuikaku*, in 1941.

66. A photograph of *Shokaku*, also dated 1941. The practice of fitting pairs of carriers with port and starboard islands was not continued in this class, and both vessels completed with small superstructures on the starboard side. As in contemporary US carriers, the bows were left open, but the hangars were totally enclosed; several major Japanese carriers were lost through bombs exploding in their hangars, resulting in uncontrollable fires fuelled by petrol vapour which could not be vented out.

67. As in the US and Royal Navies, the coming of war prompted the Japanese Navy to step up its carrier construction programme, and a large number of readily convertible merchant vessels were taken over, mainly with a view to operation on second-line duties such as transport and training. The three *Taiyo* class ships, formerly passenger liners, were employed exclusively in these roles. The name ship of the class is shown here.

67▼

▲ 68

▲ 69

68. *Chuyo*, sister-ship to *Taiyo*, in 1943. The basic work involved in converting mercantile designs to carriers was much the same everywhere: re-routing the uptakes to discharge at the sides of the ship instead of along the centreline; building a hangar on top of the hull; building a flight deck on top of the hangar; installing lifts; and equipping the vessel with defensive armament.

69. *Nisshin* was a combined seaplane carrier and minelayer along the lines of the *Chitose* class and *Mizuho* and could also handle midget

submarines, launching the latter by means of doors at the stern. A heavy armament of six 5in guns was installed forward.

70. The venerable *Furious* continued in service with the Royal Navy throughout the Second World War, little changed in appearance since the mid-1920s except for the addition of a small island superstructure, complete with pole mast and homing beacon, and a modernized armament. She is shown here operating Albacore torpedo-bombers, her forward palisades raised.

▼ 70

71▲

71. The major US fleet carrier programme of the Second World War was the *Essex* class, the first three units of which had been laid down by the time of Pearl Harbor. The ships proved exceptionally successful, and many were totally reconfigured postwar to operate fast jets. The lead ship of the class, *Essex* (CV-9), is shown here towards the end of the war.

72. Displacing about 35,000 tons in deep load condition, the *Essex*es were large, powerful carriers, capable of speeds over 30kts, and over 100 aircraft were quite frequently embarked. This is *Bunker Hill* (CVE-17), January 1945, four months before she would be very seriously damaged by Japanese kamikaze aircraft.

72▼

▲ 73

73. The *Essexes'* fixed armament was impressive, consisting of eight 5in/38 guns disposed before and abaft the island, backed up by numerous 40mm and 20mm anti-aircraft weapons (as many as 136 barrels in some ships by the end of the war) disposed in tubs and platforms wherever space allowed. The 'open bow' was retained, as seen in this view of *Yorktown* (CV-10, named thus after CV-5 had been lost in battle).

74. CV-31, identified at each end of the wooden flight deck, was *Bon Homme Richard*, shown here as completed in late 1944 with an

Avenger torpedo-bomber on deck. Visible along the port side is a deck-edge lift, a characteristic feature of the *Essex* class which has been retained in US carrier designs up to the present day.

75. *Yorktown* (CV-10) in 1943. This carrier was one of the early 'short bow' *Essexes*; later ships had their hulls lengthened forward, enabling additional AA weapons to be mounted. By this time the advent of radar was being signified by the installation of antennas atop carrier masts.

▼ 74

▲ 76

76. As a stop-gap measure pending the arrival into service of the large number of *Essex* class fleet carriers then being planned, a batch of *Cleveland* class cruisers were converted into light fleet carriers for operation by the US Navy. There were severe compromises, not least the problems involved in building a hangar and flight deck of reasonable dimensions on a narrow cruiser hull. The ships proved to be cramped, but they could support a useful air group of about thirty aircraft and they served with distinction in front-lint combat zones in the Pacific war. The photograph shows *Monterey* (CVL-26) under way.

77. The ex-*Cleveland* class carriers, known as the *Independence* class, each had a 320ft-long hangar, a small outboard island superstructure on the starboard side, and four canted funnels along

▼ 77

the deck edge to discharge boiler gases. This is *Bataan* (CVL-29), here acting as a transport, October 1944. One *Independence* class carrier, *Cabot* (CVL-28) is still (1986) in existence, serving in the Spanish Navy as *Dedalo*.

78. To assist with the training of carrier aircrews, the US Navy authorized the conversion of two paddle steamers, whose duties would be confined to the Great Lakes. One of these, *Sable* (IX-81), is shown in this June 1945 photograph. The relatively placid waters of the Lakes permitted a low freeboard, whilst the location, well away from combat zones, obviated the need for a fixed armament. Neither vessel was fitted with a hangar, nor was there a permanent aircraft complement.

▲ 79   ▼ 80

44

79. The US Navy's first two fleet carriers, *Lexington* and *Saratoga*, were still very much effective units when the Second World War broke out. *Lexington* was lost early in 1942, but her sister-ship went on to make a useful contribution to the US war effort. She had her fair share of problems, twice being torpedoed and later being badly damaged by bomb and kamikaze hits, and by the end of the war she had been relegated to training duties. She is seen here in May 1945.

80. Wartime modifications to *Saratoga* included extending her flight deck and widening it forward and aft, fitting radar equipment and strengthening her close-range battery. Her twin 8in guns before and abaft the superstructure had already been replaced with 5in mountings prior to Pearl Harbor.

81. Escort carrier construction continued apace throughout the war. Further *Bogue* class carriers were transferred to the Royal Navy, principally for anti-submarine convoy duties in the Atlantic, including *Hunter* shown here.

82. *Ravager*, like *Hunter*, was one of the eleven-ship *Attacker* class, commissioned into the Royal Navy between October 1942 and June 1943. Their low capacity (about twenty aircraft) and single-shaft, low-speed propulsion made them unsuited to the fleet role, although carriers of this class did support the Allied landings in Italy and two ships, *Fencer* and *Searcher*, took part in attacks on the German battleship *Tirpitz*.

83. Some wartime aircraft carriers were not quite what they seemed, including *Unicorn*, which served not in a combat role but as a mobile maintenance and support depot. Hangar space was sacrificed in the interests of providing extra workshops and overhaul bays, whilst the open stern enabled floatplanes to be brought aboard for servicing. In the background are the fleet carrier *Illustrious* and the battlecruiser *Renown*.

81▲

82▲   83▼

▲84   ▼85

84. The growing menace of U-boats in the Atlantic demanded more and more anti-submarine escort carriers, and another emergency programme involved the conversion of a number of tankers which became known as the *Rapana* class. One of these 12,000dwt vessels, *Amastra*, is shown here before her conversion.

85. *Amastra* configured for her role as an aircraft carrier. With her complement of aircraft carried permanently topside, the joys of maintaining the machines in mid-winter Atlantic conditions can only be imagined. The device over the bows is the framework for an acoustic hammer, intended to deal with mines.

86–89. A series of rare photographs showing *Amastra* under conversion. The original superstructure was removed, the funnel gases were vented off at the sides of the ship in the usual way, and a framework of steel girders was built up over the hull to support a full-length flight deck. No hangar was fitted, and aircraft complement was limited to four machines. The original tanker role was hardly impaired, and the ships doubled as replenishment vessels for convoy escorts.

86▲

87▲

88▲   89▼

▲90 ▼91

90. The legendary 'MAC ships' included grain carriers as well as tankers impressed by the authorities for convoy escort work. The air group consisted of four Swordfish torpedo-bombers – ideally suited for operations from small ships such as these owing to their docile handling qualities and low take-off and landing speeds – and some of the vessels had the benefit of a small hangar. Shown here is *Empire MacColl*.

91. *Empire Mackay*, with two Swordfish parked over the bows. The slim island superstructure afforded command and control of the vessel and supported basic radar antennas such as the Type 271 series surface warning system in its characteristic 'lantern' housing.

92. The *Ameer* class formed the final group of US-built escort carriers accepted for service with the Royal Navy. Individual vessels were fitted out for the specialist roles of ASW, transport or strike, but in practice there was some overlapping of duties. This photograph of *Premier* shows how closely similar these carriers were to their predecessors the *Attacker* class.

93. *Slinger* shows her flight deck configuration, October 1943. Two US-pattern 5in guns in single mountings are fitted in quarterdeck 'wings' to port and starboard; further aft, on the tip of the 'fantail', are two of the ship's eight twin 40mm Bofors AA guns. The huge radar 'mattress' is for SK air warning.

94. *Nairana* was a British-built escort carrier serving with the Royal Navy from December 1943; her heaviest defensive weapon was the sole twin 4in DP mounting at the stern, although numerous light AA weapons were also fitted.

92▲

93▲   94▼

95. *Nairana*'s sister-ship, *Vindex*, was, like her, converted from a diesel-powered fast refrigerated cargo ship and could carry up to 21 aircraft. In common with many of the war-built escort carriers, she was reconverted to a merchant ship after 1945, *Vindex* herself surviving in service until about 1970.

96. *Nairana* was commissioned into the Dutch Navy postwar, serving as *Karel Doorman* until the much more capable *Colossus* class carrier of the same name was ready in 1948. She is shown here in Dutch colours.

97. The incredible capacity of the US shipbuilding industry during the war years was fully illustrated by the programme for *Casablanca* class escort carriers; fifty ships were turned out at an average rate of one per week. The building rate was such that, towards the end of the programme, it took a mere ten weeks from keel-laying to launch, and only another month until commissioning. This is one of the first of the class, *Anzio* (CVE-57), with F4F Wildcats and a TBM Avenger aboard.

98. *Gambier Bay* (CVE-73), showing the pronounced overhang of the flight deck at the bows of a *Casablanca* class carrier. The general layout of these vessels followed that of the *Bogue*s, but two-shaft, triple-expansion reciprocating engines were fitted.

95 ▶

▼96

50

99 ▸

100 ▼ 101 ▲

99, 100. CVE-79 was *Ommaney Bay*, one of the few *Casablanca*s to be lost in action; in January 1945 she was attacked by Japanese kamikaze aircraft (photograph 100) and, too badly mauled to be worth saving, was deliberately torpedoed and sunk by a US destroyer.

101. A dramatic photograph of *Bismarck Sea*, June 1944, with two brave souls on the flight deck despite the appalling conditions. The *Casablanca*s had a nominal aircraft capacity of 28 machines; many served as aircraft transports, when their flight decks were crowded with many more.

104 ▲

102. Virtually every foot of space along the flight-deck edges of wartime US carriers was utilized, mostly for defensive 20mm and 40mm anti-aircraft guns but also, as in the case of *Makin Island* (CVE-93) here, for the stowage of life rafts.
103. A November 1943 photograph of *St Lo* (CVE-63) immediately after completion. The AA gun positions stand out along the deck-edge, where, amidships, two of the ship's four smokestacks can just be discerned. Beneath the overhanging flight deck at the stern, the single 5in gun can be seen.
104. A motley assortment forms the deck cargo of *Nehenta Bay*, (CVE-74), March 1944, including PBY Catalina amphibians, a

couple of dismantled Venturas, the fuselage of a Dakota, and a B-26 bomber. The fact that aircraft could be transported in vast quantities to the 'front line' like this was a major factor in the success of the US Pacific campaign.
105. Two further fleet carriers were completed for the Japanese Navy in mid-1942 – *Hiyo* and *Junyo*, which were originally designed as passenger liners. For the first time in Japanese carriers the funnels were incorporated into the island superstructure, canted well over to starboard to minimize the effects of corrosive fumes blowing over the flight deck. *Junyo* is shown here laid up at the end of the Second World War.

105 ▼

▲106 ▼107

108▲

106. Perhaps the most offbeat carrier of the Second World War was *Akitsushima*, built by the Japanese Navy to operate a single large flying boat. The massive handling crane at the stern gave the vessel a distinctive appearance to say the least, and her startling lines are further highlighted in this 1943 photograph by the somewhat unconventional camouflage scheme.

107. *Zuiho* in October 1944, under attack from aircraft operated by *Enterprise* (CV-6). Several aircraft carriers had their flight decks camouflaged during the Second World War, but the effectiveness of this measure was very limited: no one has yet thought of a method of disguising the wake created by a ship under way.

108. The *Commencement Bay* class represented the ultimate wartime US escort carrier design. The ships were adapted from tanker hulls, and many remained in US Navy service postwar to form the core of its anti-submarine fleet; one, specially adapted as a communications relay vessel, even served during the Vietnam War. This photograph shows that particular ship, *Gilbert Islands* (CVE-107, later renamed *Annapolis*), as she originally appeared, in 1945.

109. In order to maximize flight-deck area, the island super-structure in *Commencement Bay* class carriers, in common with other escort designs, was built out on a sponson, as shown in this view of *Vella Gulf* (CVE-111), August 1945. In contrast to the *Casablancas*, these ships were fitted with two rather than one catapult on the forward flight deck.

109▼

▲110

110. *Commencement Bay* (CVE-105), lead-ship of the class. Thirty-five vessels were originally envisaged, but the end of the war brought about a curtailment of the programme and only nineteen were actually completed, some postwar.

111. *Cape Gloucester* (CVE-109) was one of the very few

*Commencement Bay*s to see combat during the Second World War, providing air cover for US minesweeping operations during the closing stages of the conflict. She is seen her conducting sea trials, March 1945.

▼111

112. Construction of two generally similar classes of light fleet carriers was well under way in British yards by 1945, but only a handful of these ships were completed by the end of the war. One of the first was the *Colossus* class carrier *Vengeance*, which served with the British Pacific Fleet from spring 1945; she is seen here in a postwar photograph. Utilizing merchant ship scantlings, these vessels proved straightforward to build and were very successful ships: several fought with distinction in the Korean War, many were sold to overseas navies, and a few are still in service today –

including *Vengeance* herself, as the Brazilian *Minas Gerais*.
113. The two *Implacable* class fleet carriers were commissioned into the Royal Navy in mid-1944. Improved versions of *Indomitable*, they differed principally in having four- (instead of three-) shaft machinery, an extended lower hangar, and improved defensive armament. Hangar height was reduced to save weight. Both ships saw action with the British Pacific Fleet at the close of the war, *Indefatigable* (shown) receiving a kamikaze hit.

113▼

▲114

114. Italian attempts to commission an aircraft carrier were
frustrated by indecision, shortages of materials, lack of technical
expertise and, finally, the country's capitulation in 1943, but the ex-
passenger liner *Aquila* almost made it into service. Plans to rebuild
her after the war came to nothing.

115. German attempts to commission a carrier fared no better.
Incomplete at the end of the war, *Graf Zeppelin* was transferred to
Soviet authority, but in 1947 she sank whilst under tow to
Leningrad. She is seen here laid up shortly before that voyage.

▼115

116. The French carrier *Béarn* (see photographs 26 and 27) served throughout the Second World War and was not finally disposed of until the late 1960s. Her limited capabilities restricted her to support roles such as transport; this is how she appeared in early 1945.

117. The Japanese carrier force suffered not only from a shortage of ships as the Second World War began to be brought to a close – there was also an acute shortage of aircraft (and airmen to fly them) and, perhaps more importantly, of fuel. Thus, although construction continued at ever more desperate rates through until 1945, there was never much hope of getting the ships into service, even if they could be completed. *Ibuki*, shown here, was modified

from a heavy cruiser design, but she was never commissioned.

118. (Next spread) the impressive *Midway*s were the largest US carriers designed for Second World War service, although in the event the first ships missed the conflict by a matter of weeks. In a move away from earlier practice, these ships incorporated an armoured flight deck and hangar deck, although the concept of the open-sided hangar was retained. The heavy AA battery, comprising eighteen single 5in/54 mountings, was ranged along the ship at hangar-deck level. The photograph shows *Franklin D Roosevelt* (CVB-42) in September 1946; her two sister-ships, *Coral Sea* and *Midway*, still serve with the US Navy, albeit drastically modified from their original configuration.

▲119

119. The Japanese carrier *Kaiyo* did enter service, but only in a training role. A former passenger liner (her mercantile livery can be made out in this postwar photograph), she was attacked and disabled by British naval aircraft just before the end of the war.
120. *Amagi* lies at Kure as a silent memorial to the Japanese carrier force at the end of the Second World War. The product of an ambitious building scheme for sixteen purpose-built ships (*Unryu* class), she was, although completed, never deployed operationally. The first ship of the class, *Unryu* herself, did manage to get into commission, but none of the remaining vessels was ever completed.

▼120